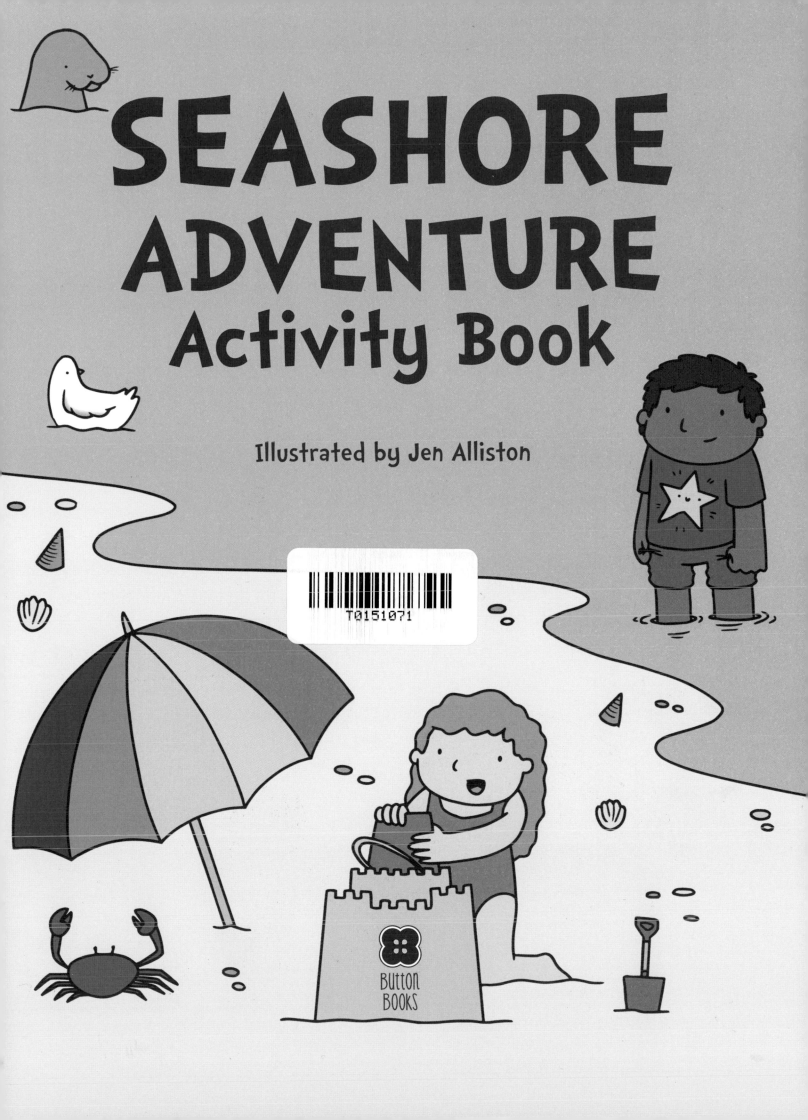

SEASHORE ADVENTURE
Activity Book

Illustrated by Jen Alliston

Button Books

We do like to be beside the sea, don't we? There is paddling to be done, wildlife to be spotted, sandcastles to be built, and ice creams to be eaten! And even when you're not actually there you can still enjoy all the fun through puzzles, jokes, and games. So turn the page and dive on in!

Get packing

Erin is packing for a trip to the beach. Check her list to see what she's forgotten.

SUNSCREEN
SUNGLASSES
TOWEL
SANDWICHES
BOOK
SUN HAT
WATER BOTTLE

Beach bound

This family is taking a trip to the beach. Help them find their way through the maze to the sea, without getting caught in a traffic jam.

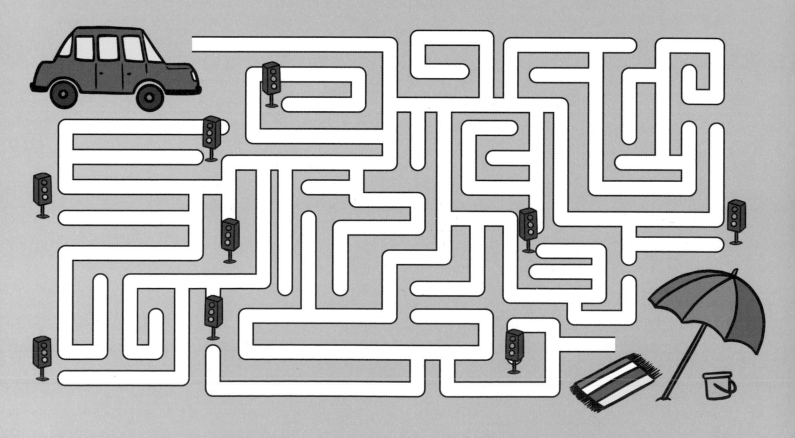

4

Aim high

Work out these problems to find out which of these sandcastles is the tallest. The highest number is the tallest castle.

5 + 9 - 2 = ⬤   8 - 1 + 7 = ⬤   4 + 3 + 2 = ⬤

Setting sail

Color in this picture of Tom and Rosie in their boat. How many fish can you spot?

Hungry gulls

Follow the lines to work out which of these seagulls is going to steal this boy's sandwich.

In the swim

Can you spot five differences between these two pictures of children swimming?

Underwater wonders

How many starfish can you spot in this picture?
Use the stickers to add some more underwater creatures to this picture.

Twice as ice

Match these ice cream cones into pairs and then color them in.

Lost seagull

This seagull has flown too far inland. Can you help her get back through the maze to the coast?

Fly the flag

This boat has a new flag but it is very dull! Draw a design on the flag and color in the rest of this picture.

Swimming pal

Join the dots to see who this girl is swimming with.

Fading castle

This sandcastle is about to get washed away by the sea. Help save it by drawing in the faded outline.

How many shells can you see?

Seal with a fish

Follow the tangled lines to see which seal catches the fish for his dinner.

Counting underwater

The sea is full of creatures that can breathe underwater. How many of the following creatures can you see?

RED FISH ◯

STARFISH ◯

CRABS ◯

JELLYFISH ◯

OCTOPUSES ◯

Sunny times

Can you spot five differences between these pictures of a girl relaxing on the beach?

Picnic picks

Who has the most sandwiches?

Fun in the sun

Color in this picture of people having fun on the beach.

Mixed-up ices

These ice creams have got mixed up. Can you work out what flavors they are? Then color them all in.

MELARAC
_ _ _ _ _ _ _

TINM
_ _ _ _

NILVALA
_ _ _ _ _ _ _

HERCRY
_ _ _ _ _ _

TECHOLOCA
_ _ _ _ _ _ _ _

ASPRERBRY
_ _ _ _ _ _ _ _ _

Throw party

Work out the problems to see who can throw their beach ball the furthest. The one with the highest number is the winner.

2 + 3 + 8 =

6 + 7 - 4 =

5 + 1 + 6 =

Beach bound

Use the stickers to help these children get ready for a day at the beach.

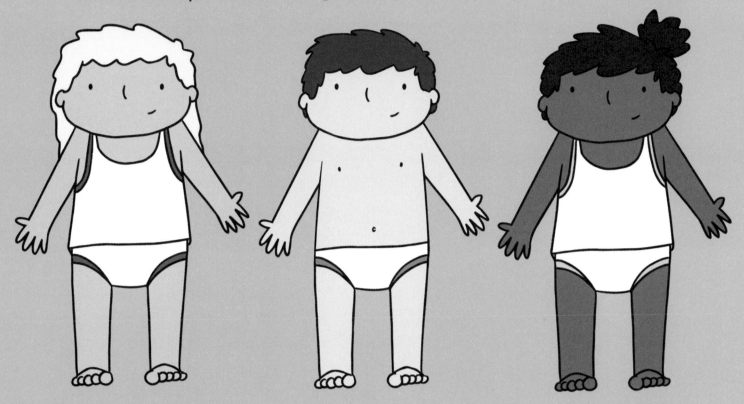

Fishing for differences

Can you spot five differences between these two pictures of a fishing boat?

Fishy friends

Use some stickers to add fish to this underwater scene.

Starfish snack

You'll need:

 Paper

Knife

 Peanut butter

 2 raisins

Scissors

Pencil

 Slice of bread

Banana

1. Cut out a piece of paper the same size as the slice of bread.

2. Draw a star on the paper following the steps below.

3. Cut out the star shape to make a template.

4. Put the template on the bread and score around it with a knife.

5. Cut out the star shape.

6. Spread peanut butter all over one side of the star.

7. Add slices of banana and raisins to make eyes.

8. Enjoy!

18

Ask a grown-up to help!

Dotty yacht

Join the dots to complete this sailing picture.

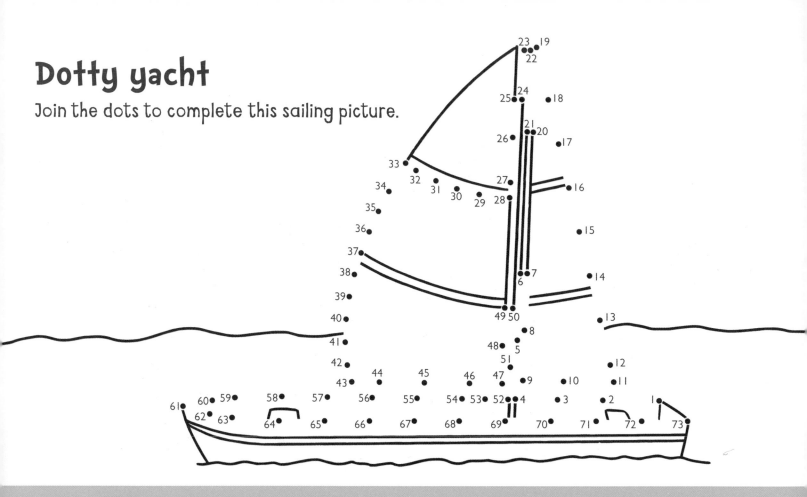

Mixed-up creatures

Can you work out what these mixed-up sea creatures are? Then find the right sticker to put next to the name.

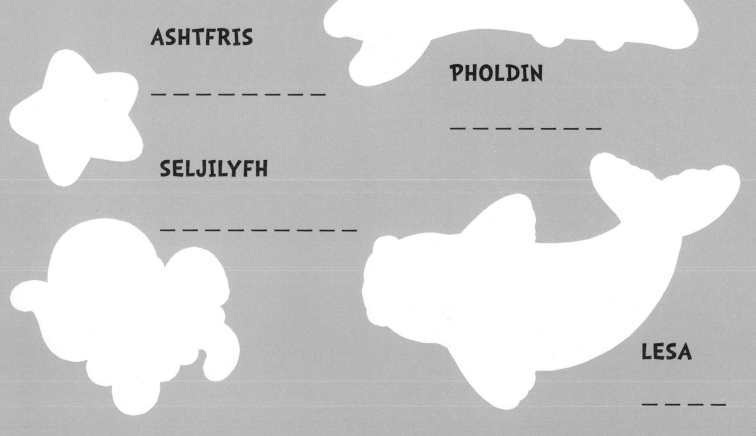

ASHTFRIS

_ _ _ _ _ _ _

PHOLDIN

_ _ _ _ _ _ _

SELJILYFH

_ _ _ _ _ _ _ _

LESA

_ _ _ _

Oddballs

Can you spot the two beach balls that are different to the others?
Then color them all in.

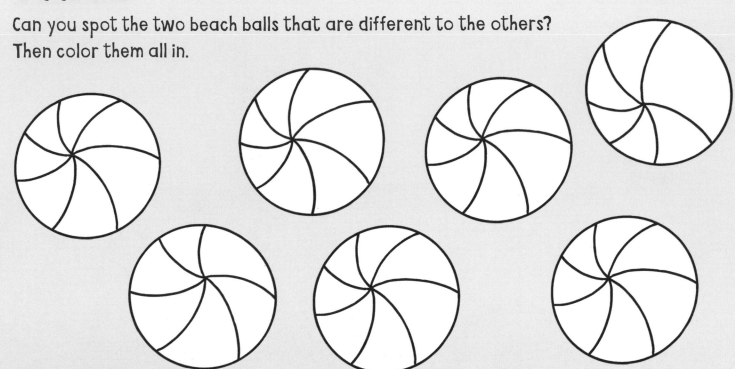

Join the pack

A family is packing for a trip to the seashore. Which of these things do they need to take with them and which should they leave at home?

TOWEL ☐

BEACH BALL ☐

PICNIC BASKET ☐

TV ☐

BUCKET AND SPADE ☐

LAWN MOWER ☐

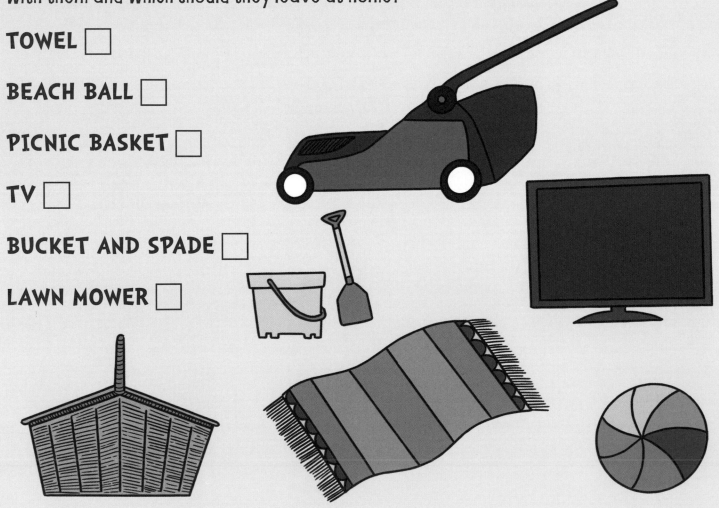

Lost letters

Some letters have fallen off these beach signs. Can you work out which ones go where?

LI_EGUAR_
ON DU_Y

NO FI_HIN_

W_RNING!
ST_ONG CURRE_T

N_ S_IMMING
AFTER DAR_

A
R
N
O
W
K
F
D
T
S
G

Match making

Draw lines to match these swimmers to their beach bags.

Sea creature wordsearch

Can you find these hidden words?

SEAL

SEAGULL

CRAB

JELLYFISH

STARFISH

CORAL

MUSSEL

CLAM

OCTOPUS

DOLPHIN

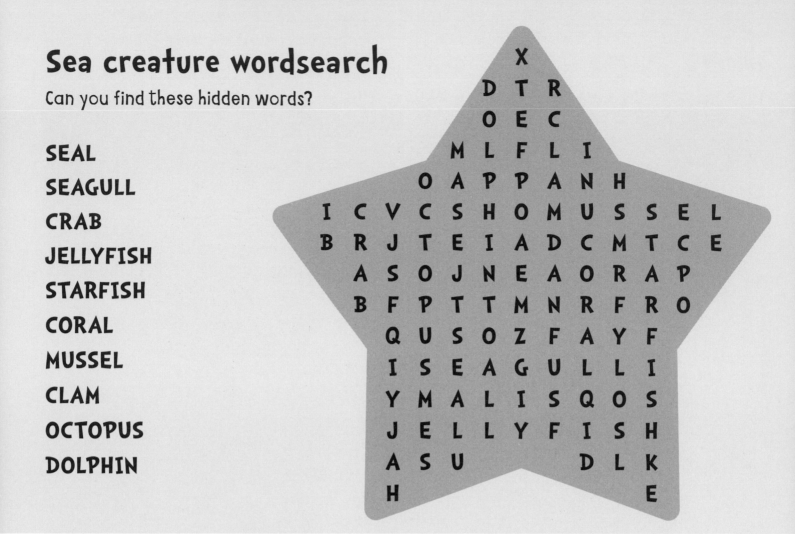

Disappearing diver

This diver is slowly disappearing the deeper she goes! Draw around her to bring her back into view, then color the picture in.

What's missing?

There's something missing from each of these seashore activities. Find the right sticker to complete each picture.

Double beach fun

When a length of sand links an island to the mainland, it is called a tombolo. Where this happens you have waves coming in on both sides, as if two beaches have been joined together! Add stickers to this tombolo scene to bring it to life.

Draw a beach hut

You'll need:

Eraser

Paper

Pencil

Coloring pens or pencils

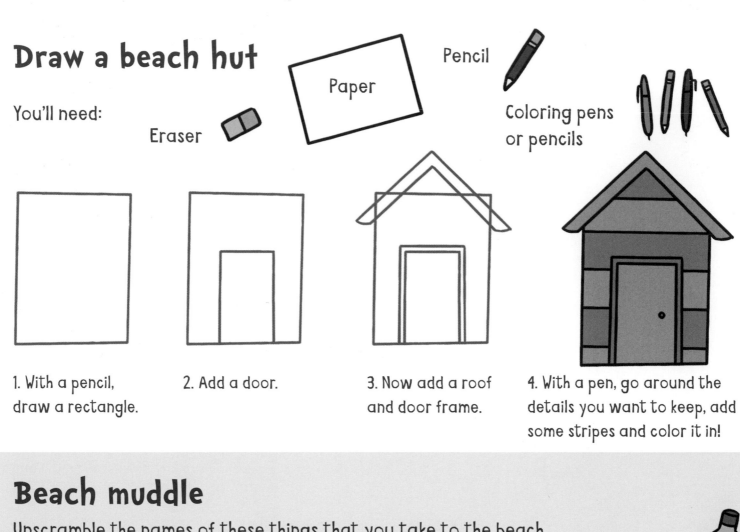

1. With a pencil, draw a rectangle.

2. Add a door.

3. Now add a roof and door frame.

4. With a pen, go around the details you want to keep, add some stripes and color it in!

Beach muddle

Unscramble the names of these things that you take to the beach.

This protects you from the sun and helps to stop you getting painful sunburn.

ENSENSUCR _ _ _ _ _ _ _ _ _

You use this to get dry after you've been swimming.

OWLET _ _ _ _ _

You wear these to protect your eyes when the sun is bright.

SALESUSNGS _ _ _ _ _ _ _ _ _ _

This is like an umbrella but you use it to protect you from the sun.

OLPARAS _ _ _ _ _ _ _

These are nice to wear on a hot day.

THOSRS _ _ _ _ _ _

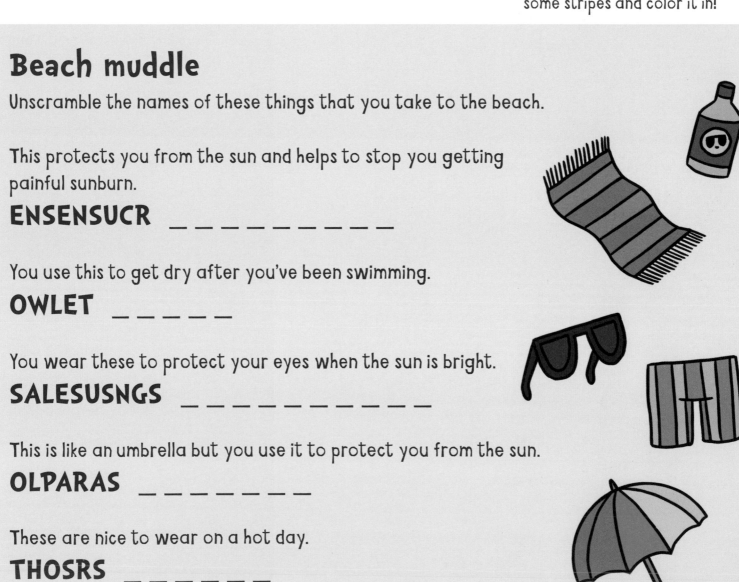

Merry mermaids

Can you spot five differences between these two pictures of mermaids?

Game mix-up

Follow the lines to work out who is playing with what.

Sundae best

Make these boring ice creams into sundaes by adding stickers.

Message in a bottle game

Sometimes people find bottles washed up on beaches with messages hidden inside them, put there long ago. Here's a game you can play so you can find one too.

1. One player writes a letter, poem, or story on a piece of paper, rolls it up and puts it in a bottle.

2. They then hide it somewhere and draw a map to show where it is.

3. Using the map, the other players try to find where the bottle is hidden.

4. Whoever finds it gets to read the message and add their own to the bottle, so the game starts over again.

5. If you're playing the game on a beach, remember to take your bottle and messages home with you at the end of the day.

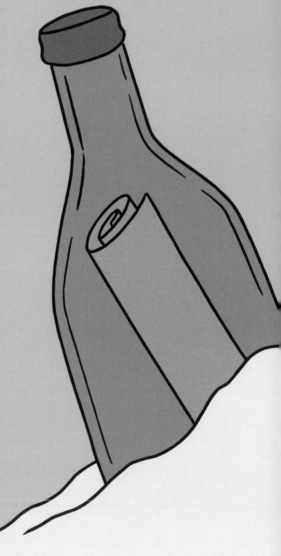

Disappearing pier

This pier is fading away into the sea mist. Draw around it to bring it back into view and then color it in.

Sandal mix-up

These beach shoes have gotten all mixed up. Draw a line between the pairs of shoes. Which is the odd one out?

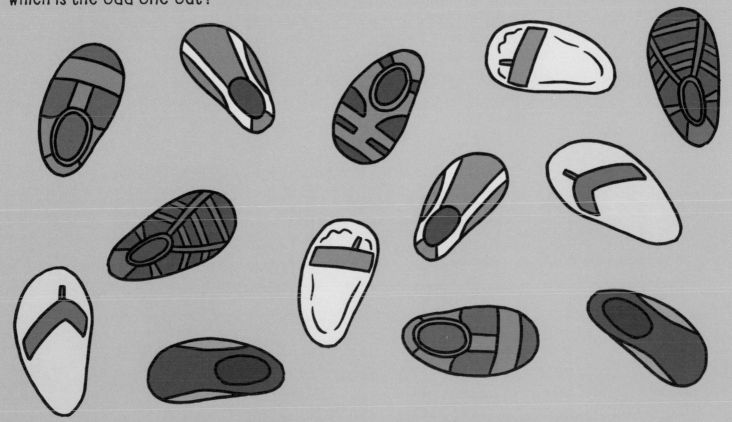

Hidden creatures

There are lots of creatures hiding in this rock pool. How many of each can you spot?

SEA ANEMONES

CRABS

BARNACLES

PERIWINKLES

MUSSELS

STARFISH

JELLYFISH

Dotty crab

Join the dots to reveal this snappy crab.

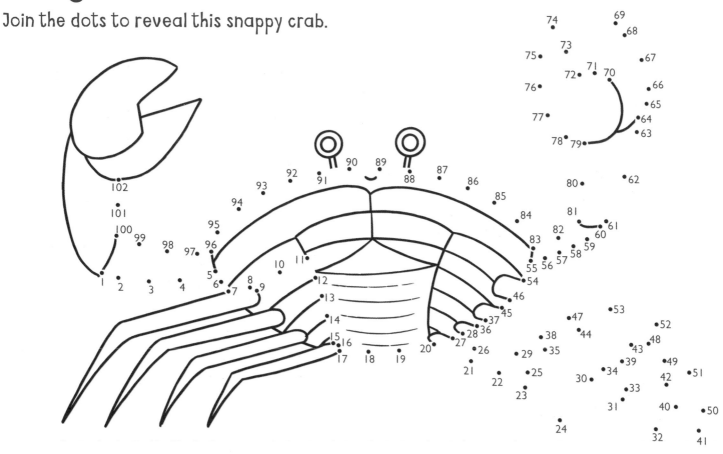

Make a splash

Which of these swimmers has won prizes for diving? They've got brown hair, a stripy swimsuit, and a patterned towel.

Pair of castles

Can you spot which two of these sandcastles are exactly the same?
Then color them all in.

Seashore wordsearch

Can you find these hidden words?

LIFEGUARD

SANDCASTLE

PICNIC

BOAT

SHELL

WAVES

ICE CREAM

SNORKEL

```
          E   C       I
      G   P   R   M   X
  R   P   C   V   B   F   W   A   T
  L   I   F   E   G   U   A   R   D
  H   C   T   D   E   F   V   Y   S
  K   N   L   W   S   J   E   L   N
  E   I   B   H   H   T   S   R   O
  J   I   C   N   W   E   P   R   V   R   D
  E   C   S   P   K   L   S   T   F   K   P
  Y   E   T   V   M   L   J   O   L   E   M
  T   C   O   N   L   G   I   Q   D   L   B
I   E   M   R   S   C   P   G   F   E   T   R   P       F
H   L   R   J   E   K   G   M   O   Q   V   G   L   W   R   S   T
D   B   M   S   A   P   Y   H   Z   T   P   R   C   B   O   A   T
M   S   C   H   M   L   S   A   N   D   C   A   S   T   L   E   M
```

SEA

BOTTLE

PAPER

REPLY

WRITE

AGE

TOWEL

ADDRESS

MESSAGE

MEET

LETTER

TOUCH

STAMP

PADDLING

GANNET

OCTOPUS

SEAL

STARFISH

CRAB

Tidy-up time!

These friends are heading home after a day at the beach, but they've left five things behind. Can you help find everything so that they don't leave the beach in a mess?

A bottle in the ocean

Choose words from the sticker pages to complete this story.

Eva and Ben love to visit the beach. One day they were [ ] in the sea

when they spotted a bottle bobbing by. "People shouldn't throw things into the

[ ]!" said Eva. "Let's get it out."

So they waded over and pulled the bottle out. It was then that they noticed it looked

very old and had a piece of [ ] inside it. It was a [ ] in a

bottle! Very excited, the children took the bottle and dried it on their [ ].

They took the message out and began to read...

'To whoever finds this message: I would love a pen pal. Please [ ] to me at

this address and tell me about yourself.'

The message was from someone called Violet and the [ ] was in a

country far away across the ocean. Then they noticed the date - the letter had been

written 40 years ago!

34

When they got home, Eva and Ben sat down to write a [   ] to Violet. Then they waited every day to see if a [   ] came. Just when they had almost forgotten all about it, a letter with a foreign [   ] arrived! Inside was a lovely letter from a lady who had thrown the bottle in the sea when she was around Eva and Ben's [   ]. 'I wouldn't throw a [   ] in the sea now,' she wrote, 'because that's pollution, but 40 years ago we didn't realize that.'

Now Eva and Ben keep in [   ] with Violet by email. Maybe some day they'll get to [   ] her in person.

Odd hut out

Can you spot which of these beach huts is the odd one out? Then color them all in.

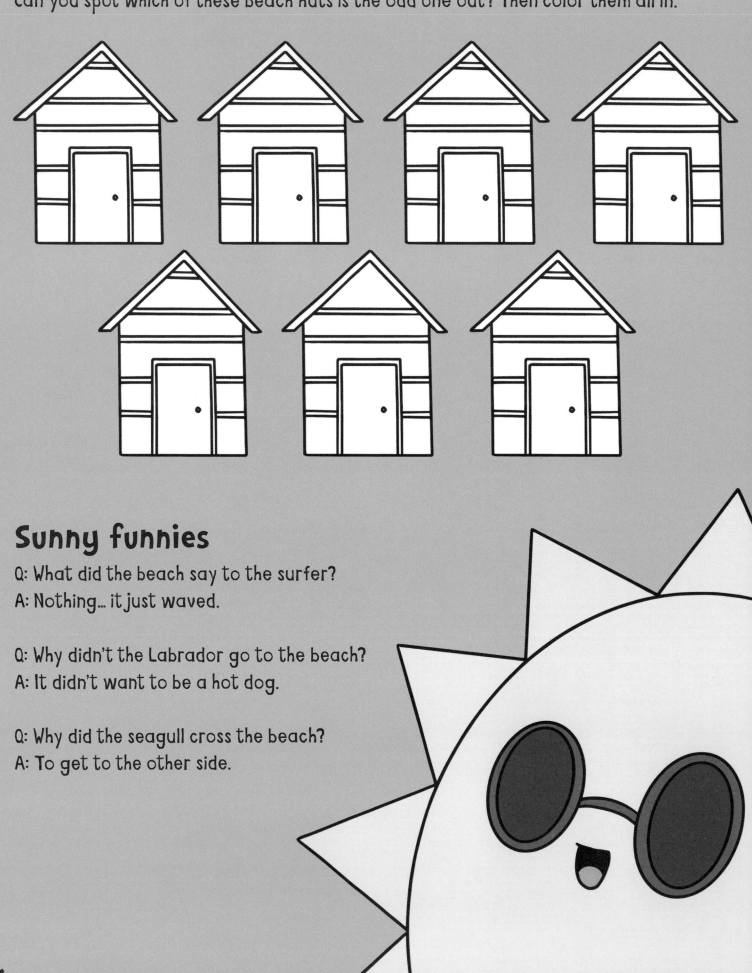

Sunny funnies

Q: What did the beach say to the surfer?
A: Nothing... it just waved.

Q: Why didn't the Labrador go to the beach?
A: It didn't want to be a hot dog.

Q: Why did the seagull cross the beach?
A: To get to the other side.

Creature match

Can you match the names of these sea creatures to their descriptions?

STARFISH   **OCTOPUS**

SEAL   **CRAB**

GANNET

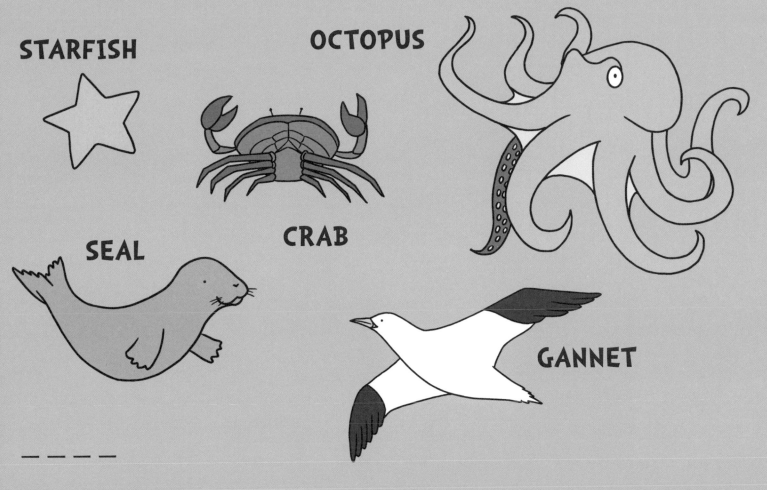

_ _ _ _

I'm covered in a protective shield, with pincers for pinching anyone who bothers me.

_ _ _ _ _ _ _

I'm very intelligent and best known for having eight limbs.

_ _ _ _

Despite being a great swimmer, I'm not a fish. I like to sleep on land.

_ _ _ _ _ _ _ _

Named after my shape, I hold tight to rocks under the sea. I'm very good at healing and can regrow whole limbs if I ever lose one.

_ _ _ _ _ _

I fly high above the water until I spy a fish with my excellent eyesight. Then I dive like a bullet into the water and catch it for my lunch.

Draw a crab

You'll need:

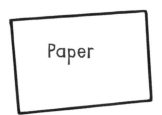
Paper

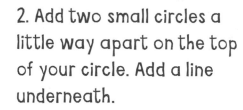
Eraser

Pencil

Coloring pens or pencils

1. Draw a circle in the middle of your piece of paper.

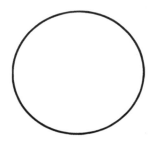

2. Add two small circles a little way apart on the top of your circle. Add a line underneath.

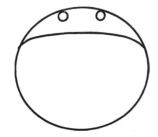

3. Draw a small circle in the middle of each eye. Fill in the larger parts with black pen. Draw stalks below each eye.

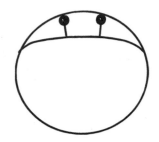

4. Add some antennae next to the eyes.

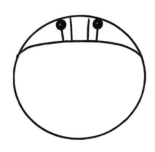

5. Draw a small oval either side of the crab and bigger ones above them.

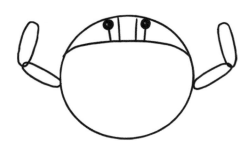

6. Add claws by drawing curved lines as shown.

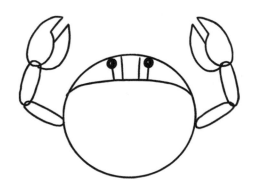

7. Draw crescent shapes to make four legs on either side at the bottom of your crab and a belly.

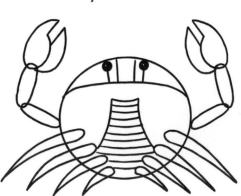

8. Now draw over the outline with a black pen and color your crab in.

Beach kit wordsearch

Can you find these hidden words?

TOWEL

BEACH BALL

SUNGLASSES

CANOE

SANDALS

SUNSCREEN

SUN HAT

PARASOL

```
          R L O
      P H G M S F A
    K T B C E U S C V
  H R S B B N N M A J Q
D T E U L E F H Y N T V S
K T J N P A R A S O L D A
G O E S M C D T D E F P N
F W B C M H B R S F N K D
L E F R S B E C J W D J A
T L Z E G A J S R R W K L
P Y H E R L D B C C T L S
  S U N G L A S S E S M
    P P B Y D L M D K
      L F I S C U R
        T Y Q
```

Rock on

Can you spot five differences between these two pictures of a rock pool?

Mixed-up skiers

These waterskiers have got tangled up! Can you work out who is with which boat?

Surf's up

Which of these surfers has ridden the biggest wave? Work out the problems to find out. The highest number equals the biggest wave.

2 + 10 + 3 =   9 + 7 - 5 =   1 + 8 + 3 =

All the fun

Color in this picture of people having fun on the pier. How many pairs of sunglasses can you count?

41

Letters making a splash

Complete these words using the letters from the word WAVES.

_OLLEYBALL

PAR_SOL

_URF

J_LLYFISH

_ATER

Shore giggles

Q: What is the strongest creature in the sea?
A: A mussel.

Q: Where do fish sleep?
A: On the seabed.

Q: Which part of a fish weighs the most?
A: The scales.

Mirror images

Draw in the other half of these beach creatures.

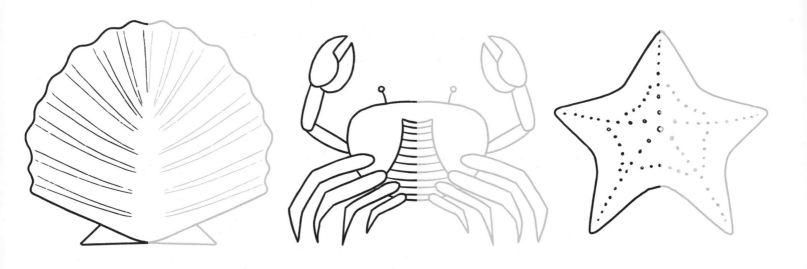

Dotty mermaid

Join the dots to see this lovely mermaid.

Beach counting

How many of the following can you spot in this picture?

BEACH BALLS

KITES

SNORKELS

BUCKETS

SPADES

Forgotten snacks

Tom made a list of all the treats to bring for his picnic, but he seems to have forgotten something. Can you work out what it is?

SANDWICHES

STRAWBERRIES

YOGURTS

COFFEE

CAKE

COOKIES

APPLES

Make a boat

You'll need:

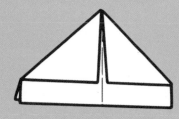

Paper

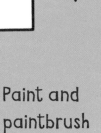

Pen

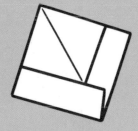

Paint and paintbrush

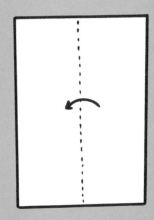

1. Fold your paper in half vertically and open it out again.

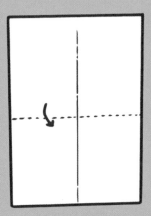

2. Now fold it in half the opposite way.

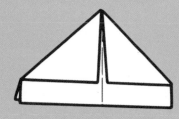

3. With the edges at the bottom, fold both the top corners into the middle.

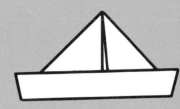

4. Fold up the bottom edges at the front and back.

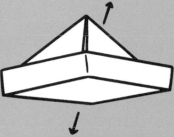

5. Put your thumbs inside the shape and pull the front and back apart.

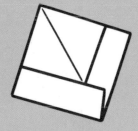

6. Flatten the shape neatly.

7. Fold the bottom points up at the front and back to make a triangle shape.

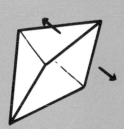

8. Pull the front and back apart, then flatten.

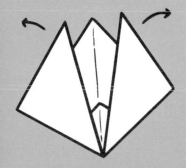

9. Pull the side flaps outwards.

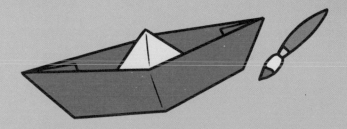

10. Paint your boat and write a name on it in pen.

Changing tides

Have you noticed that sometimes you visit the same beach but it looks different? This is because of tides, which are constant changes in sea levels. These pictures show the same jetty at high tide and low tide. Look at the differences and color the pictures in.

Sail shadows

Can you work out which of these sailboats matches this silhouette?

Fish figures

Which of these anglers has caught the most fish? Work out the problems to find out.

12 - 4 + 3 = ◯   2 + 8 - 1 = ◯   5 + 7 + 6 = ◯

Jumbled picnic

Peter has dropped his picnic and now it is all mixed up. Can you rearrange the letters to help him out?

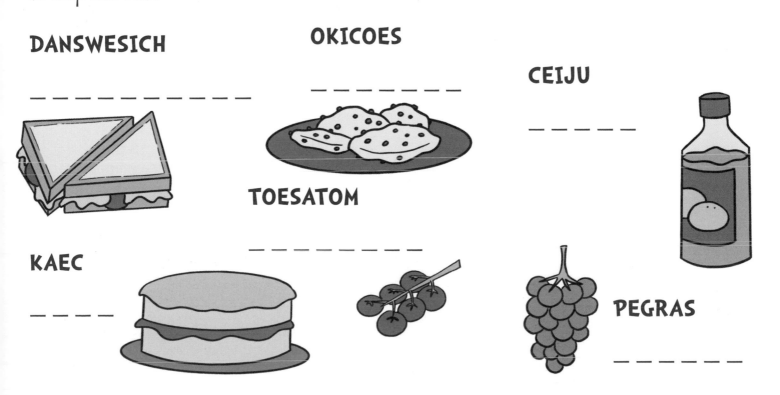

DANSWESICH

_ _ _ _ _ _ _ _ _

OKICOES

_ _ _ _ _ _ _

CEIJU

_ _ _ _ _

TOESATOM

_ _ _ _ _ _ _ _

KAEC

_ _ _ _

PEGRAS

_ _ _ _ _ _

Teddy's sunglasses

You'll need:

Tape measure

Scissors

Teddy

Pencil

Cardstock

Coloring pens

Elastic

Ask a grown-up to help!

1. Measure the width of your teddy's head.

2. In pencil, draw a line that length along the edge of your piece of cardstock.

3. Draw two curved shapes next to the line to make a B.

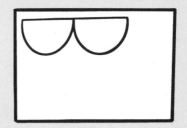

4. Now draw D shapes within each curve.

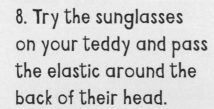

5. Fill in the frame area with your favorite color and color the D-shaped areas with a dark pen.

6. Cut the B shape out. Make a small hole in each side with the pencil.

7. Thread the elastic through one side and tie a knot to hold it.

8. Try the sunglasses on your teddy and pass the elastic around the back of their head.

9. Thread the elastic through the hole on the other side and pull it so it will hold the glasses in place. Tie a knot to secure. Now your cool teddy will be the talk of the beach!

48

Beach laughs

Q: What happens when you throw a green rock into the Red Sea?
A: It gets wet.

Q: What did the magician say to the fisherman?
A: Pick a cod, any cod.

Q: What do you call a fish without any eyes?
A: Fsh.

Shell pairs

Draw lines to match these pairs of shells and then color them in. Can you spot the odd one out?

Dune to the sea

Audrey is on her way to the beach for a paddle. Help her find her way through the sand dunes, down to the water's edge.

Activity wordsearch

Can you find these beach activities hidden in the grid?

PADDLING

SWIMMING

SURFING

SAILING

VOLLEYBALL

RUNNING

CANOEING

FISHING

```
            F H J
    V B G M P S R R F
      O K T L A A M M I
        O L S U R F I N G S R
      M I L W W B J L P P H G R
      R N E I H F C I B B I E U
      Y T Y M S Z N N P D N M N
    P B C B M A V H G L L G B N F
    R B S A I C C M M K P P Q I B
    C R L L N K R S S Y W M N N G
    L D D L G F P A D D L I N G K
            C A N O E I N G J
              U A P
```

Towel art

The pattern on this beach towel has faded. Add your own design and then color it in.

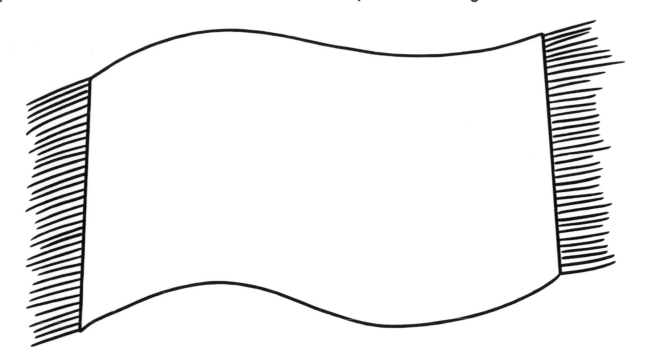

Dotty octopus

Join the dots to complete this picture of a jolly octopus.

Faded message

This message found in a bottle has got a bit hard to read in places. Can you work out what letters are missing and write them in?

> To whoever f_nds this m_ss_ge:
> I have been sh_pwrecked on a
> de_ert island! Please come and
> resc_e me. I'm on a _eart-shaped
> island, south of Pe_u. Hurry!
> Sam x

Jelly peril

Help this swimmer get back to the beach, avoiding the jellyfish on the way.

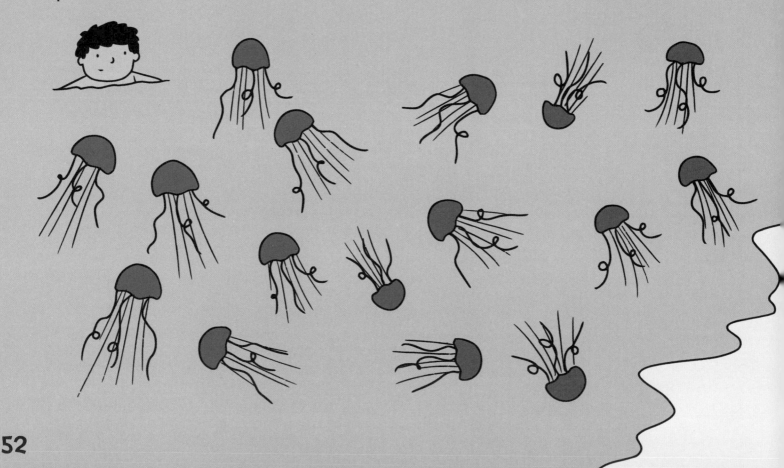

52

Safe in the sun

These friends are having fun on the beach, but they haven't protected themselves from the sun properly. Use stickers to add parasols, sunglasses, sun hats, and sunscreen to the picture.

Matching urchins

Can you match up these pairs of sea urchins and spot the odd one out?

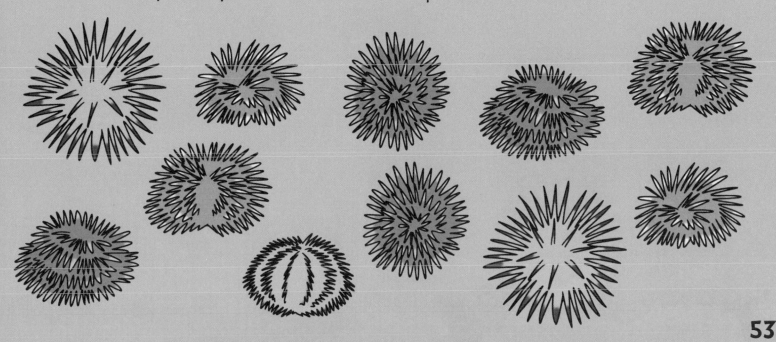

Fair fun

Can you spot five differences between these two pictures of a funfair on a pier?

Ice eater

Which of these friends ate the most ice cream? They have brown hair, red shorts, and a stripy T-shirt.

Marine party

Color in this picture of mermaids having fun.
How many lobsters can you see?

Make a sandcastle without sand

You'll need:

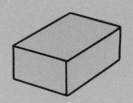

Cardboard box

4 cardboard tubes

Glue

Paintbrush

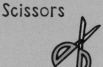

Scissors

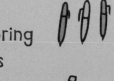

Coloring pens

Pencil

Sticky tape

Paper

Sand-colored paint

1. Turn your box upside down. In the four corners, draw around the end of your cardboard tubes.

2. Cut out the circles in the corners.

3. Make small cuts about ³/₈in (1cm) deep around the ends of the tubes.

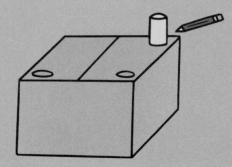

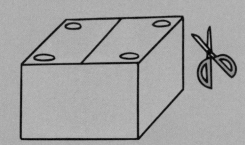

4. At one end of each tube, cut across the base of alternate tabs.

5. Push the other ends into the holes in the top of the box. Spread out the cut ends and secure with tape.

6. Paint your box and tubes with sand-colored paint.

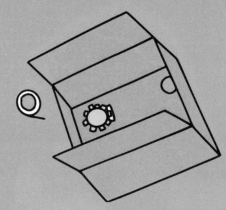

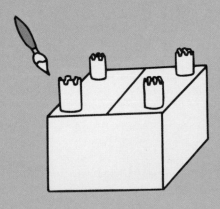

7. On a piece of paper, draw shells and other shapes to decorate your sandcastle. Color them in.

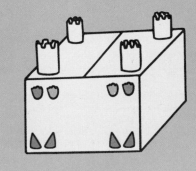

8. Cut out the shells and shapes and stick them all over your castle to decorate it.

56

Stay safe

Lifeguards watch that everyone stays safe in the water. Can you spot five differences between these pictures of a lifeguard at work?

Fishy tails

Use stickers to add tails to these sea dwellers.

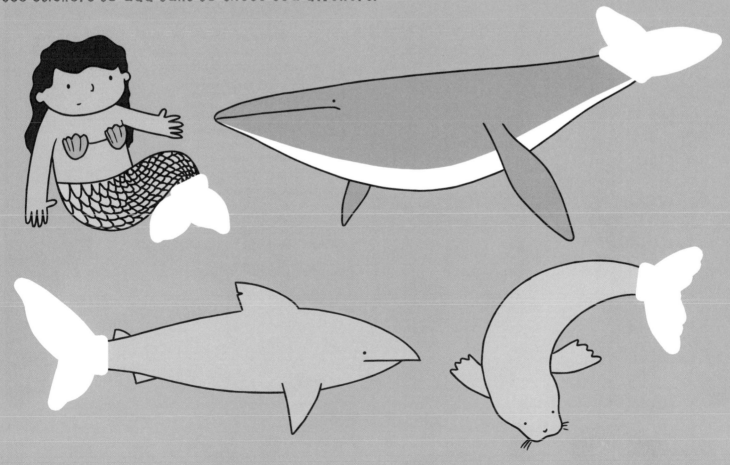

Get packing (page 4)

She's forgotten the sandwiches.

Beach bound (page 4)

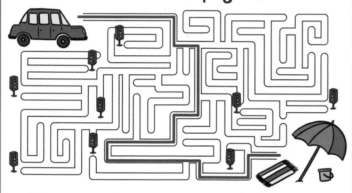

Aim high (page 5)

12   14   9

Setting sail (page 5)

There are 12 fish.

Hungry gulls (page 6)

In the swim (page 6)

Underwater wonders (page 7)

There are 11 starfish.

Twice as ice (page 8)

Lost seagull (page 8)

Fading castle (page 10)

There are 17 shells.

Seal with a fish (page 10)

Counting underwater (page 11)

Red fish – 2   Jellyfish – 4
Starfish – 11   Octopuses – 2
Crabs – 5

Sunny times (page 12)

Picnic picks (page 12)

3   4   2

Mixed-up ices (page 14)

MELARAC CARAMEL
TINM MINT
NILVALA VANILLA
HERCRY CHERRY
TECHOLOCA CHOCOLATE
ASPRERBRY RASPBERRY

Throw party (page 14)

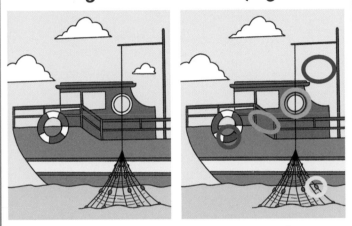

13   9   12

Fishing for differences (page 15)

Mixed-up creatures (page 19)

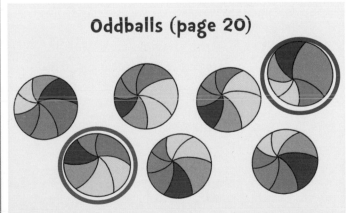

ASHTFRIS STARFISH
PHOLDIN DOLPHIN
SELJILYFH JELLYFISH
LESA SEAL

Oddballs (page 20)

Join the pack (page 20)

TOWEL ☑   TV ☒
BEACH BALL ☑   BUCKET AND SPADE ☑
PICNIC BASKET ☑   LAWN MOWER ☒

Lost letters (page 21)

LIFEGUARD ON DUTY

NO FISHING

WARNING! STRONG CURRENT

NO SWIMMING AFTER DARK

Match making (page 21)

Sea creature wordsearch (page 22)

What's missing? (page 23)

Beach muddle (page 26)

SUNSCREEN
TOWEL
SUNGLASSES
PARASOL
SHORTS

Merry mermaids (page 27)

Game mix-up (page 27)

Sandal mix-up (page 29)

Hidden creatures (page 30)

Sea anemones - 6   Mussels - 6
Crabs - 7   Starfish - 6
Barnacles - 10   Jellyfish - 4
Periwinkles - 8

Make a splash (page 31)

Pair of castles (page 32)

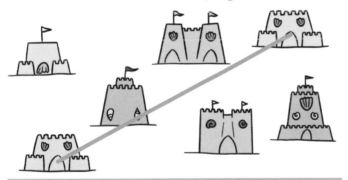

Seashore wordsearch (page 32)

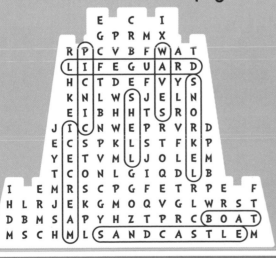

Tidy-up time! (page 33)

Odd hut out (page 36)

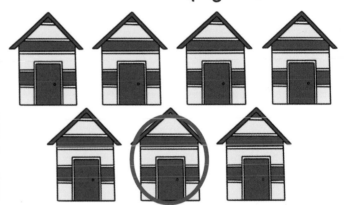

Creature match (page 37)

CRAB

I'm covered in a protective shield, with pincers for pinching anyone who bothers me.

OCTOPUS

I'm very intelligent and best known for having eight limbs.

SEAL

Despite being a great swimmer, I'm not a fish. I like to sleep on land.

STARFISH

Named after my shape, I hold tight to rocks under the sea. I'm very good at healing and can regrow whole limbs if I ever lose one.

GANNET

I fly high above the water until I spy a fish with my excellent eyesight. Then dive like a bullet into the water and catch it for my lunch.

Beach kit wordsearch (page 39)

Rock on (page 39)

Mixed-up skiers (page 40)

Surf's up (page 40)

15 **11** **12**

All the fun (page 41)

There are 5 pairs of sunglasses.

Letters making a splash (page 42)

VOLLEYBALL JELLYFISH
PARASOL WATER
SURF

Beach counting (page 44)

Beach balls – 3 Buckets – 3
Kites – 1 Spades – 4
Snorkels – 3

Forgotten snacks (page 44)

He's forgotten the yogurts.

Sail shadows (page 46)

Fish figures (page 47)

11 **9** **18**

Jumbled picnic (page 47)

DANSWESICH **SANDWICHES** OKICOES **COOKIES** CEIJU **JUICE**
TOESATOM **TOMATOES**
KAEC **CAKE** PEGRAS **GRAPES**

Shell pairs (page 49)

Dune to the sea (page 50)

Activity wordsearch (page 50)

```
            F H J
    V B G M P S R R F
    O K T L A A M M I
  O L S U R F I N G S
  M I E W W B J L P H
  R N Y I H F C I B I
  Y T M S Z N N P D N
P B C B M A V L G B G
R B S A I C C M M K P
C R L L N K R S S Y W
L D D L G F P A D D L
    C A N O E I N G J
        U A P
```

Faded message (page 52)

To whoever finds this message:
I have been shipwrecked on a
desert island! Please come and
rescue me. I'm on a heart-shaped
island, south of Peru. Hurry!
Sam x

Matching urchins (page 53)

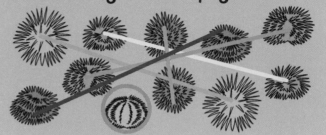

Fair fun (page 54)

Ice eater (page 54)

Marine party (page 55)

There are 8 lobsters.

Stay safe (page 57)

Fishy tails (page 57)

First published 2021 by Button Books, an imprint of Guild of Master Craftsman Publications Ltd, Castle Place, 166 High Street, Lewes, East Sussex, BN7 1XU, UK. Text © GMC Publications Ltd, 2021. Copyright in the Work © GMC Publications Ltd, 2021. Illustrations © 2021 Jennifer Alliston. ISBN 978 1 78708 096 6. Distributed by Publishers Group West in the United States. All rights reserved. The right of Jennifer Alliston to be identified as the illustrator of this work has been asserted in accordance with the Copyright, Designs, and Patents Act 1988, sections 77 and 78. No part of this publication may be reproduced, stored in a retrieval system, or transmitted in any form or by any means without the prior permission of the publisher and copyright owner. While every effort has been made to obtain permission from the copyright holders for all material used in this book, the publishers will be pleased to hear from anyone who has not been appropriately acknowledged and to make the correction in future reprints. The publishers and author can accept no legal responsibility for any consequences arising from the application of information, advice, or instructions given in this publication. A catalog record for this book is available from the British Library. Publisher: Jonathan Bailey. Production: Jim Bulley and Jo Pallett. Senior Project Editor: Wendy McAngus. Managing Art Editor: Gilda Pacitti. Color origination by GMC Reprographics. Printed and bound in China. Warning! Choking hazard—small parts. Not suitable for children under 3 years.